Managing
Your Boss

Sandi Mann

BARRON'S

All inquiries should be addressed to:
Barron's Educational Series, Inc.
250 Wireless Boulevard
Hauppauge, NY 11788
http://www.barronseduc.com

Library of Congress Catalog Card No. 2001025287

International Standard Book No. 0-7641-1950-8

Library of Congress Cataloging-in-Publication Data
Mann, Sandi.
    Managing your boss/Sandi Mann.
      p. cm.—(Business success series)
    Originally published: London: Hodder & Stoughton Education, 2000.
    Includes index.
    ISBN 0-7641-1950-8
    1. Managing your boss. I. Title. II. Series.
HF5548.83 .M364 2001
650.1'3—dc21

                                  2001025287

PRINTED IN HONG KONG
9 8 7 6 5 4 3 2 1

Contents

◆

Introduction

◆

The title *Managing Your Boss* is sure to raise eyebrows among many workers; after all, isn't it supposed to be the boss who manages them, not the other way around? Yet the theme running through this book is that the relationship between boss and employee should be two-way—employees who want to get ahead should "manage" their boss as much as their boss will be managing them. Workers do not need to be passive recipients of their boss's demands or expectations, but rather, partners in the process through which mutually beneficial goals are achieved.

The first step to managing your boss is to understand her. Research suggests that managers generally have a particular psychological makeup, and appreciating this will help you understand what drives and motivates them and what makes them tick.

The next step involves the establishment of a "psychological contract" that is made up of those normally unspoken agreements that govern expectations between boss and employee. A natural progression of the psychological contract is the art of impression management; this is a skill that, when developed, will help ensure that you are—or at least appear to be—everything your boss wants you to be. In this way, you keep your boss happy and she will then be more motivated to keep you happy. However, in order for her to keep you happy, your boss needs to know what you want—getting more from your boss is therefore the next crucial step and will ensure that you will never again be unable to ask for a raise or promotion.

The steps outlined above do assume that you have a fairly reasonable boss, but what happens if you are unfortunate enough to have the boss from hell? The next section deals with three of the most difficult boss–subordinate situations, while the final section deals with troubleshooting more mundane problems.

Following all these steps should ensure that you are well equipped to manage your boss effectively in almost every situation and should therefore help you on the road to becoming a terrific boss yourself.

---

1. *What kind of animal is the "boss"?*

2. *What type of boss do you have?*

3. *Using the psychological contract to manage your boss*

4. *How to impress your boss*

5. *Getting more from your boss*

6. *Dealing with the boss from hell*

7. *Common problems with managing the boss*

Chapter 1

What Kind of Animal Is the "Boss"?

Before we can really talk in any detail about how to manage your boss, it is helpful to gain a better understanding of what sort of person your boss might be. If you can appreciate and understand your boss's makeup, you will be far better equipped to manage her. In this chapter we will examine the general qualities that managers must have in order to perform effectively as a "boss." Then we will look more closely at the specific qualities your own boss might have or the type of manager that she might be.

The following issues are covered.

---

1. Discovering what your boss does all day

2. Knowing what skills your boss has

3. Your boss's attitude toward you

4. Understanding what motivates your boss

WHAT DOES YOUR BOSS DO?

Most managers or leaders take on a huge variety of tasks; supervising you might be just a small part of their wide-ranging responsibilities. An average manager will spend about a third of her time and effort on traditional management activities such as planning or decision making, a third on communication activities, including paperwork, and the rest on human resource management activities, such as motivating or training staff, and on networking activities. Knowing how your boss is likely to spend her time allows you a valuable insight into her mind since you will have a better idea of the sort of concerns that may preoccupy her. This is important, since many people seem unable to see much beyond their own view of their boss, in which the boss performs only tasks that are relevant to them as individuals. Yet only a tiny percentage of the work your boss does is likely to directly impact on you, which means that any tasks you perform for her or any requests you make will need to fit somehow into the broader world of your boss's authority. This is worth bearing in mind later when we will look at ways to work more intelligently with your boss.

QUALITIES OF A BOSS
In order to perform effectively in each of the above areas, your boss will need to draw upon a wide range of skills, including

◆ the ability to allocate tasks appropriately among staff members.

◆ the ability to project authority and to take responsibility.

◆ excellent time-management and organizational skills.

◆ the ability to act on her own initiative and be self-motivated.

◆ skill in fostering team spirit.

◆ motivational skills.

◆ "people" skills such as empathy.

◆ communication skills so that she can relate and talk to people at different levels, both senior and subordinate to herself.

◆ the ability to delegate.

These skills are ones that bosses can learn throughout their career, but many depend on an underlying psychological makeup. Not everyone aspires to be a boss, nor is everyone capable of taking on the role. Psychologists have identified several personality traits or personal qualities that constitute the "makeup" of a manager, and your boss is likely to have some or all of them. Understanding the psychological makeup of your boss will allow you greater insight into what makes her tick. She should be

◆ *sensitive* enough to "read" people and situations. She should be able to notice when people are unhappy at work or ready for more challenges, or when events might mean that changes are needed in the workplace.

◆ *analytical* and good at problem solving. Many people turn to the boss for solutions and although some of these will depend on training and experience, much will depend on an inborn aptitude for lateral thinking.

◆ *decisive.* Even in school some children are able to make quick decisions, while others are unsure of themselves and their abilities to choose the right path. The boss should have the self-confidence to go with any decisions she makes.

◆ *socially competent.* She should be able to communicate at different levels, listen appropriately, draw people out, and behave with suitable social etiquette in a variety of scenarios.

◆ *emotionally resilient* so that she can bounce back when knocked down and does not let it affect her confidence or decision-making abilities.

◆ *proactive.* Such people do not wait for things to happen or come to them, but actively try to make things happen or initiate their own projects.

◆ *creative.* Bosses are often creative people who are able to view things from various angles and come up with creative solutions or plans that stretch or go beyond previously established limits.

These qualities, therefore, make up the personality profile of the ideal boss. However, if your boss has *all* these qualities, you probably don't need to read this book. Not all bosses will, of course, be the same, and will vary in the degree to which they possess these traits. It is likely that the missing or weaker traits are the reasons that problems occur between employees and the boss. In addition, a great deal of the boss's managerial style will depend not only on personal qualities and skills, but also on her inherent attitude toward human nature and behavior.

YOUR BOSS'S ATTITUDE TOWARD YOU

In very general terms, the way bosses treat people depends on their attitude toward human nature and behavior. There are two opposing attitudes that bosses may take:

Carrot-and-stick attitude

The assumptions that managers will make if they hold this attitude are that

◆ the average person is inherently lazy and dislikes work.

◆ most people need to be coerced, controlled, directed, or even threatened if the organization is to achieve its goals.

◆ the average person avoids responsibility, lacks ambition, and works only for the financial security.

Bosses who hold these attitudes thus believe that rewards and sanctions are the only way to achieve organizational aims, so their job is to be authoritative and directive.

Cooperate and trust attitude

On the other hand, managers who hold this set of attitudes toward people have the following assumptions:

◆ Most people are self-motivated to work and want to enjoy it.

◆ Coercion is unnecessary if people are given tasks that meet their own objectives as well as those of the company or organization.

◆ Most people can be trusted to complete tasks without continual supervision.

◆ People work for reasons other than financial security.

The boss who holds these attitudes thus believes that the best way of managing is to elicit cooperation from her team and create conditions that will ensure that people want to work hard and achieve organizational as well as personal goals.

WHAT MOTIVATES THE TYPICAL BOSS?

Psychologists have identified five different dimensions that motivate or drive people in their lives. These motivations or needs exist in different amounts in different people so that one person may have high needs on one dimension but not on another. These needs are

◆ *the need for achievement (n-Ach)*. People who are highly motivated by a need for achievement are concerned with accomplishments and compete strongly against others.

◆ *the need for affiliation (n-Aff)*. People who are highly motivated by a need for affiliation are concerned about establishing, maintaining, or restoring close, personal, emotional relationships with others.

◆ *the need for power (n-Pow)*. People with a high n-Pow are motivated by winning a debate or argument, controlling or dominating others.

◆ *the need for autonomy (n-Aut)*. Adults high on the n-Aut are motivated by completing tasks without assistance from others.

◆ *the need for activity inhibition (n-ActI)*. People motivated by n-ActI are driven to do things for the greater good of a company or organization, even at the expense of their own personal desires or needs.

So, which of these needs is your boss most motivated by? Successful leaders in organizations and companies have been found to be most likely to have

---

High n-Pow

High n-ActI

Above average n-Ach

Low n-Aff

Low n-Aut

That is, your average boss is likely to be highly motivated by a need for power or control, by a desire to act for the greater good of the organization or company, and by some need for personal achievement. She is less concerned with building strong relationships with subordinates (such as you) or working on her own.

However, remember that this is the profile of the *average* boss and your own boss may have a different pattern of motivations. Once you have a good idea of what motivates her, you will then be able to act in ways that concur with these motivations. For instance, if your boss is high n-ActI, she may expect the same from you and will not appreciate your appearing to put your own needs or goals before those of the organization or company. A boss with a high n-Aut will not appreciate unrequested input from you. And, a boss low in n-Aff will not be anxious to socialize with you or spend time and energy cultivating a friendship with you—so don't make her feel uncomfortable by trying to "affiliate" with her.

SUMMARY

We have started by examining the profile of a typical boss. This is a crucial first step to managing your boss since it is only by understanding her psychological makeup that you can really begin to understand how to get along with her as a boss. Now we will see a more in-depth analysis of your own boss in terms of her managerial style, as well as practical pointers for handling each type of boss.

Chapter 2

What Type of Boss Do You Have?

Now we will focus on a more individual diagnosis of the type of boss you have in order to understand him. There are many ways to classify people, and the different types discussed in this section are just some of the approaches you could take. It is worth noting that your boss may not fit neatly into any one category—rather, he should be "classified" according to the type or category that most accurately resembles him.

The main features, therefore, are

---

1. diagnosis of your boss in terms of his leadership style.

2. diagnosis in terms of his thinking style.

3. quizzes to diagnose your own boss.

4. tips for managing each type of boss.

LEADERSHIP STYLES

Leadership styles refer to the way in which the functions of your boss or manager are carried out or the way in which your boss typically acts or behaves toward you.

The following are some typical leadership styles:

1. *Dictatorial.* This boss feels that he is in charge because he is the best person for the job and therefore his job as leader

is to tell others what to do and how to do it. Such a boss is often motivated by n-Power (see page 8) and finds it difficult to see things from other people's points of view. He tends to rely on reward and punishment in order to get the best out of his workers.

2. *Bureaucratic.* This boss got where he is today by following the rules, and sees no reason to have a different philosophy now. He tends to lack entrepreneurial risk-taking qualities, but he is likely to be a law-abiding and reliable citizen who takes his responsibilities very seriously. Any queries from subordinates, problems to be solved, or decisions to be made are dealt with by referring to the rulebook. Such managers like to have everything written down, and use forms and paperwork excessively to keep track of what's happening.

3. *Charismatic.* This boss motivates his followers by inspiring them to achieve the company's goals rather than pursue their own interests. This boss leads by personal example and is likely to

gain great loyalty and hard work from his team. Such a boss is often himself motivated by a high n-ActI (see page 8).

4. *Consultative.* The consultative boss may be high on n-Aff (see page 7) and is likely to involve and consult his team at every and any opportunity. Decisions are made with input from staff and changes to the status quo are discussed thoroughly. Such a boss may be afraid of alienating staff or even of taking the plunge and making solo decisions; he may lack the courage of his convictions and prefer to share the burden somewhat.

5. *Laissez-faire.* The genuine laissez-faire boss is the manager who observes that members of the team are working well on their own and need little input. This boss makes a conscious decision to leave them to it without interfering and is happy and comfortable doing so. He is likely to have a "cooperate and trust" attitude (see page 7).

6. *Abdictatorial.* This boss differs from the laissez-faire one in that, in this case, the boss simply does not care enough to get involved

with his team's problems. He leaves them to it, not out of trust, but because he wants to avoid problems and difficult situations. The staff is left to make decisions and deal with problems that really ought to be the responsibility of the boss.

Quiz to diagnose your own boss's leadership style

◆ Do your colleagues seem to vie for your boss's attention?   3

◆ Does your boss often tell you what to do, rather than ask you?   1

◆ Does your boss seem unable to make innovative decisions?   2

◆ Do you feel that you can approach your boss about any problems?   4

◆ Do you feel that your boss does not involve you in decisions?   1

◆ Do you feel that your boss lacks creativity?   2

◆ Does your boss show little interest in your views?   1

◆ Does your boss contribute only when asked to?   6

◆ Do you often find that changes are made or practices introduced without your consultation?   1

◆ Does your boss stick rigidly to the rules?   2

◆ Does your boss leave you to proceed with minimal input?   6

continued

15

◆ Do you feel that you want to work hard to please
  your boss? 3

◆ Does your boss seem uninvolved except when
  problems arise? 6

◆ Does your boss withdraw rewards if necessary? 5

◆ Does your boss discourage you from coming to him
  with problems? 6

◆ Does your boss often talk about visions and dreams
  for the company? 3

◆ Is your boss well liked and well respected by most
  people? 3

◆ Does your boss involve you in most decisions? 4

◆ Is your boss often preoccupied with other things? 6

◆ Are there regular team meetings to discuss new
  issues? 4

◆ Does your boss often appear inflexible? 2

◆ Does your boss rarely introduce anything new
  without consulting you? 4

◆ Does your boss seem uninterested in what you are
  doing? 6

◆ Is your boss happy to hand over tasks to others? 6

◆ Do you sometimes feel that you have too much
  responsibility? 6

Analysis of quiz answers	Number of "Yes" Answers
1 = Dictatorial	_____
2 = Bureaucratic	_____
3 = Charismatic	_____
4 = Consultative	_____
5 = Laissez-faire	_____
6 = Abdictatorial	_____

(Note: Your boss may not score in any one style but may be a mix of two or three styles.)

TIPS ON MANAGING THE BOSS ACCORDING TO HIS LEADERSHIP STYLE

Manage the *dictatorial* boss by

◆ building his trust in you.

◆ asking his permission before doing anything.

◆ keeping him well informed with progress reports.

◆ demonstrating that you are carrying out orders willingly and with enthusiasm.

Manage the *bureaucratic* boss by

◆ submitting any requests in writing.

◆ not expecting any diversion from the rules.

◆ supplying him with the rules when necessary to help him make a decision.

◆ keeping written records of everything.

Manage the *charismatic* boss by

◆ being enthusiastic about his dreams and visions.

◆ demonstrating that you put the company before your own concerns.

◆ showing loyalty to your boss and company.

◆ demonstrating a belief in his plans and ideas.

Manage the *consultative* boss by

◆ being anxious to share in decision-making processes.

◆ not being afraid to give your opinion.

◆ giving encouragement and praise to your boss.

◆ involving your boss in social activities such as trips to the cafeteria at lunch or after-work drinks.

Manage the *laissez-faire* boss by

◆ showing that you can be trusted to get on with tasks.

◆ sending memos to inform him of your progress.

◆ seeking help only when problems arise.

◆ not bothering him with trivial concerns or issues.

Manage the *abdictatorial* boss by

◆ getting go-aheads for projects in writing.

- ◆ putting any problems that arise in writing.

- ◆ requesting formal meetings to discuss issues.

- ◆ turning to others for input where possible.

THINKING STYLES

Have you ever wondered why there are some people you can talk to and understand easily, but others who seem to rub you the wrong way or who always seem to misunderstand your best intentions? These differences may reflect the various thinking styles we each have. Thinking style has to do with the way we prefer to think or how we process information. Several different ways of processing information have been identified, leading to a variety of thinking styles. Many of these can be used to differentiate and diagnose the type of boss that you have, and enable you to work to help rather than hinder his preferred style of working. The following shows some of the thinking styles your boss might prefer.

1. *The detail-conscious boss.* This boss prefers to process information in small bite-sized chunks. He is able to pay a great deal of attention to detail and is very thorough and tenacious. Along with a preference for receiving information in these small chunks, he also likes to disseminate it this way, which can be frustrating if you have a larger chunk size than he. The detail-conscious boss may think of time in terms of days, weeks, and months, rather than years.

2. *The big-chunk boss.* The big-chunk boss likes to have an overview or general impression of a topic and is less interested in the minor details. He can become quite impatient if anyone tries to give him too much detail. This boss is good at thinking in the

long term or developing an overall strategy, and is usually a fast processor simply because he tends to gloss over the less important details.

3. *The left-brain boss.* The boss with a left-brain dominance has a preference for order and logic. He is very organized and focused and likes to finish a task once he starts it. He also prefers to work on one task at a time rather than multitask. This type of boss probably writes things down a lot and has excellent time-management systems.

4. *The right-brain boss.* This boss is big on multitasking and will often be found doing several jobs at once. Things seem much more chaotic around the right-brain boss, who may have an untidy desk, papers everywhere, and be forever panicking over deadlines. He is always forgetting things, he is not big on lists, and he relies on carrying information in his head, which is a mistake because his brain is less able to distinguish between jobs that he has done and those he has only thought about doing.

5. *The reactive boss.* This boss is thoughtful and cautious and pre-occupied with the consequences of any decisions he makes. This is why he often prefers to stay with the status quo rather than rock the boat with an idea or plan that might go wrong. However, he is good at responding to problems, needs, or requests from his team, although he might require so much information before deciding on a course of action that subordinates become frustrated with the slow response.

6. *The proactive boss.* The proactive boss is an initiator who loves to start new projects, although he doesn't always manage to finish them before getting excited about the next one. In his enthusiasm to get going with a new idea or project, he may fail to

survey the alternatives carefully enough, or pay enough attention to detail.

7. *The sameness boss.* The sameness boss likes familiarity and stability, so he does not respond well to change. He has a low tolerance for difference and is likely to notice and reject what is new. This boss is likely to be older and have been in his position for many years, neither seeking promotion nor a new direction. He tends to be quite set in his ways and resistant to innovation.

8. *The differences boss.* This boss, on the other hand, embraces change and new ideas. He encourages fresh approaches from his team and is always looking for new ways of working. He is likely to move around in different jobs a lot and is constantly seeking promotion and new direction. The differences boss may often reorganize his team but show little interest in mundane or repetitive aspects of the team's tasks.

QUIZ TO DIAGNOSE YOUR BOSS'S THINKING STYLE

◆ Does your boss take a long time to complete a task, paying attention to every detail?   1

◆ Is your boss easily distracted?   4

◆ Does your boss prefer to work on one task at a time?   3

◆ Does your boss often seem impatient when you are explaining things?   2

◆ Is your boss quite cautious?   5

continued

◆ Does your boss resist routine work? 8

◆ Is your boss very organized? 3

◆ Does your boss dislike being disturbed while working? 1

◆ Does your boss have a neat and well-organized office? 3

◆ Is your boss uninterested in the details, preferring the whole picture? 2

◆ Does your boss insist on knowing every little detail about projects you are involved in? 1

◆ Does your boss often seem to be doing several things at once? 4

◆ Does your boss worry a great deal about the consequences of any decisions? 5

◆ Does your boss tend to leave things to the last minute? 4

◆ Does your boss like information to be cut to the bottom line? 2

◆ Is your boss good at repetitive or perennial tasks? 7

◆ Does your boss get excited by the latest fad or innovation? 8

◆ Does your boss delegate the routine or mundane work to others? 8

◆ Does your boss seem, at times, overly demanding? 1

◆ Does your boss have a regular routine? 7

◆ Does your boss seem forgetful and need reminding about details?   4

◆ Is your boss full of ideas?   6

◆ Does your boss prefer to have time to think things through before making a decision?   5

◆ Is your boss rarely late for meetings, and does he dislike people who are?   3

◆ Does your boss resist change?   7

◆ Does your boss love to start new projects?   6

◆ Does your boss seem less interested in finishing a task than in starting the next?   6

◆ Does your boss often have a vision or long-term strategic plan?   2

◆ Does your boss always seem to be changing things?   8

◆ Does your boss sometimes seem unable to consider the consequences of his actions?   6

◆ Does your boss prefer to work on existing projects rather than start new ones?   7

◆ Is your boss unlikely to make snap decisions?   5

Analysis of quiz answers	Number of "Yes" Answers
1 = Detail-conscious boss	_____
2 = Big-chunk boss	_____
3 = Left-brain boss	_____
4 = Right-brain boss	_____
5 = Reactive boss	_____
6 = Proactive boss	_____
7 = Sameness boss	_____
8 = Differences boss	_____

(Note: Your boss may straddle two or more categories.)

TIPS ON MANAGING YOUR BOSS ACCORDING TO HIS THINKING STYLE

Manage the *detail-conscious boss* by

◆ regularly giving him lots of information.

◆ making everything as clear as possible.

◆ giving him lots of written updates.

◆ not disturbing him when working; make prearranged meetings.

Manage the *big-chunk boss* by

◆ giving him a general overview of projects rather than all the details.

◆ trying to take care of the small details for him.

◆ using bullet points or marking or highlighting key points in reports.

◆ talking long-term instead of day-to-day.

Manage the *left-brain boss* by

◆ presenting thoughts and ideas logically.

◆ arriving on time for meetings.

◆ meeting deadlines.

◆ not approaching him with too many issues or concerns at once.

Manage the *right-brain boss* by

◆ helping him with time management.

◆ offering help as deadlines approach.

◆ writing important points down for him.

◆ giving him lots of gentle reminders of things.

Manage the *reactive boss* by

◆ making sure he is fully informed.

◆ helping him think through any consequences of any decisions you want him to make.

◆ giving your boss plenty of time and space to make decisions.

◆ showing that you have considered every eventuality.

Manage the *proactive boss* by

◆ approaching him with exciting new ideas.

◆ helping complete tasks that bore him.

◆ becoming excited by his ideas.

◆ surveying all alternatives—so he doesn't have to.

Manage the *sameness boss* by

◆ pointing out how new tasks are similar to old ones.

◆ helping with decision making by reminding him of a precedent.

◆ resisting the temptation to suggest a lot of new ideas.

◆ helping him cope with change by suggesting a gradual change rather than a quantum leap.

Manage the *differences boss* by

◆ pointing out how different new ideas are from old ones.

◆ thinking laterally.

◆ bringing new ideas to his attention.

◆ reacting positively to change.

SUMMARY

In this chapter we have been concerned with diagnosing your boss in terms of his leadership and thinking style so that you can identify those tips that will best help you manage him. Now we will turn our attention to the psychological contract that you can develop in order to be sure you meet your boss's needs and expectations.

Chapter 3

Using the Psychological Contract to Manage Your Boss

You have your written contract, or you should—your boss should give you a contract within 12 weeks of your initial employment, but the most important step toward managing your boss is to develop a psychological contract. This is simply an unwritten agreement about the expectations you both share. For instance, the boss's expectations of the employee may be that the employee will work hard, not clock-watch, be loyal to the company, accept training or transfers, and perform some undesirable tasks. In return, the employee might expect the boss to provide training or growth opportunities, promotion prospects, reasonable working conditions, and (at least until recently) security—in today's delayered and slimmed-down corporate climate, promises of security have been replaced with promises of skills training to help make the employee employable elsewhere. Establishing a psychological contract avoids many of the misunderstandings that people commonly have with their boss; personally, it means that you can successfully manage your boss by meeting her needs, wants, and expectations.

Psychological contracts, almost by their very definition, are voluntary, subjective, dynamic, and informal, and as such, it is virtually impossible to spell out all the details formally at the time the written contract of employment is made.

In this chapter we will examine the areas your psychological contract should cover, before looking at how to go about establishing such a contract with your boss. Topics include

1. communications.

2. progress reports.

3. working pattern.

4. level of proactivity.

5. professional development.

6. how to establish the psychological contract.

COMMUNICATIONS

The whole key to managing your boss is to meet her expectations; make her happy and she will be more inclined to keep you happy. Communication is a key area and managing this aspect can make or break your relationship with the boss. When you are establishing your psychological contract, you should aim to have the following questions answered:

◆ Which means of communication does your boss prefer?

◆ How frequently does your boss want to hear from you?

◆ Does your boss want to hear about every issue or just major problems?

◆ How does your boss want to hear about your achievements?

◆ How can you expect to receive communications from your boss?

◆ Does your boss expect a response to every communication?

Means of communication
The communication medium that your boss prefers may depend on what you wish to communicate. The choices are phone, including voice mail, face to face (which can be in an arranged meeting or an ad hoc by-the-coffee-machine basis), written memo, or e-mail. It is important to establish the preferred medium before you start bombarding your boss with daily e-mails, only to find she never logs on or receives 120 e-mails a day. As a general rule, use the guide on page 31.

PROGRESS REPORTS

For this section, it will help to refer back to Chapter 2 in order to understand what kind of boss you have. Her attitude toward progress reports and updates will probably depend largely on her leadership and thinking style. However, the beauty of establishing a psychological contract is that this is one area where you do not need to use guesswork—you can simply ask her. And ask her

Means of Communication

Medium	Best for	Psychological contract Check that:
Phone	Important issues requiring an immediate response	Your boss doesn't mind being disturbed at such times.
E-mail	Queries that don't need a quick response, issues you want your boss to be aware of (including your achievements) and that you are happy to form a written record of. (You should be aware that e-mails may end up printed out and put in your file.)	Your boss uses e-mail but doesn't get so many that there is no time to read them all.
Memo	When you want to use a different medium from your usual one to emphasize a point—memos should not be used too frequently. Also used to attach to another document or report you are submitting.	Your boss does not dislike bits of paper floating around and clogging her In box.
Formal meeting	Complex issues that need face-to-face contact.	Your boss expects the occasional face-to-face meeting and will make time for you when you request one.
Ad hoc face to face	Quick, spur-of-the-moment issues that arise just as the boss appears.	Your boss doesn't mind being hassled every time she wanders down to the cafeteria.

you must, because this is an area that can lead many a boss to lose confidence in her workers—she may feel that she does not know what they are doing. When it comes to information concerning the progress of projects, there are generally three types of bosses.

1. the boss who wants to be kept informed of every stage

2. the boss who is happy just to receive the finished product

3. the boss who likes occasional updates

Find out, during the psychological contract-setting stage, what kind of boss yours is, so that you can meet her expectations. Once you know about the expected frequency of communication, you will need to establish the preferred medium of communication, and this may be different for progress reports than for other types of communication. For instance, many a boss who prefers e-mails for general communication purposes expects formally typed reports for updates on progress.

WORKING PATTERN

Unless your official contract is very specific about your required working pattern—and many jobs now do not have strictly defined hours; the days of clocking in and out are gone for many skilled workers—your psychological contract should cover these aspects. Certainly, with new patterns of working becoming more and more popular, the chances are that you will need to determine some answers to the following questions.

◆ Am I expected to be in the office at a certain time in the morning?

◆ Am I expected to be at my desk by a certain time?

◆ Am I expected to work late, and if so, how often?

◆ Am I expected to work weekends?

◆ Are my hours flexible?

◆ Can I work from home, and if so, how often?

◆ If I am not at my desk—for example, out with a client—am I expected to tell you where I am?

◆ Do you want to know my whereabouts at all times in advance?

It should be stressed here that most of these questions should not be asked explicitly since there may not be any easy answers your boss can give. Rather, they are questions that you should be attempting to find answers to during the process of establishing the psychological contract that will be discussed later. In addition, explicit answers may not tell the whole story. For instance, a boss may *say* that working late is not necessary, but may be secretly impressed by the late worker. It is your task to find the real answers, not the given ones.

In general, you should be aware of the issues outlined on page 35 regarding work patterns when establishing your psychological contract (see also the following chapter's material on impressing your boss).

LEVEL OF PROACTIVITY

How proactive does your boss expect you to be? Does this match the level of proactivity that you would like in your job? These are the sorts of questions you need to find answers to in your psychological contract. Some bosses expect their staff to sit at their desks and wait for the work to come to them. Such bosses do not encourage creativity and innovation and are probably found in the sort of industry where routine and mundane tasks make up the bulk of the work. On the other hand, more and more bosses expect staff to be proactive to some degree and go out and find work or look for ways of improving the status quo. Similarly, some employees would rather just get on with tasks assigned without having to worry about being proactive, while others feel that this would

Work Patterns

Arriving early	The boss is usually impressed by this because it demonstrates how hardworking you are. But be aware that a psychological contract is two-way and it might not suit you to be up at the crack of dawn every day. Come to some compromise with yourself. (Note: Check that your boss is in to witness your early starts if this is the whole point of them!)
Working late	Again, the boss is likely to be impressed, but be careful. Working late too often can lead many bosses to think that you are a slow or inefficient worker. Find the right balance.
Working weekends	This a point that can be explicitly agreed upon between you and your boss. See Chapter 5 for the rights you have regarding weekend work.
Flexitime	Many workers love the idea of flexitime; for instance, they can avoid the rush hour or take the kids to school. But be careful that your flexible hours do not compromise your visibility; make sure you do not miss meetings or key events that might take place before you arrive.
Working from home	The main thing to be aware of here is visibility; if you are home based for some or all of the week, you are not around to be seen working or for informal but valuable networking opportunities. Your boss may say she is OK with your being home based but may feel insecure about what you are doing when you are out of sight. Counter this by agreeing in the psychological contract to keep your boss more informed of progress than an office-based worker would.
Diaries	Keeping these either in advance or retrospectively is a good idea. If your boss does not want them, agree in your psychological contract that you will keep them yourself. They are a valuable record of what you have been doing and when, especially if yours is not the sort of job with easily measured work outputs.

stifle their creativity. Establish the level of proactivity your boss desires according to the following hierarchy:

Level 1 **Total reactivity**. The boss expects you to complete assigned tasks only; no need for proactivity.

Level 2 **Reluctant proactivity**. Here the boss will allow you to be proactive only when your assigned tasks are completed.

Level 3 **Partial proactivity**. This boss encourages proactivity although a reasonable portion of work will be assigned tasks that must be completed as well.

Level 4 **Majority proactivity**. Here, it is expected that most of your work will be self-generated, with only the occasional task being assigned by the boss.

Very often, the level of proactivity the boss expects will be implicit rather than explicitly stated; this is why the psychological contract is so important—it helps bring implicit expectations to the forefront of consciousness.

PROFESSIONAL DEVELOPMENT

It is in the area of personal professional development that the concept of a psychological contract is best known. Historically, the whole idea of a psychological contract was tied up with the expectations an employee had of the employer in terms of career development: I will work hard for you and in return you will give me reasonable job security, promotion prospects, and the skills to make me marketable to other firms. This contract has changed dramatically over the years as the idea of jobs for life has disintegrated with the advent of downsizing, globalization, and increased competition from new markets. Now, it is unreasonable to expect your employer either to offer you a job for life or even to manage your career development. Instead, a new psychological contract should be drawn up in which you, the employee, pledge to take responsibility for your own career development, while the employer agrees to provide you with the training or experiences necessary to make you more marketable.

It is therefore important to get your boss to commit to helping you with your continuing professional development. For your part, you should identify gaps in your skill, knowledge, or experience base, and identify opportunities to fill those gaps. The aim of your psychological contract is to gain your boss's consent for you to take advantage these opportunities through attendance at training courses, contributing to or performing new tasks, or learning new skills.

ESTABLISHING THE PSYCHOLOGICAL CONTRACT

Now that we know what a psychological contract should consist of, we can turn our attention to devising or establishing such a contract. The important point to remember is that the psychological contract differs from the formal contract in that

1. it is not explicit.

2. it is rarely written.

3. it is very informal.

4. it may not be established prior to starting the job or even within the first few weeks.

5. it is not binding.

6. it has no legal element.

The process of establishing the psychological contract can begin when you start a new job, but equally can be started at any point. Use the following guide to help:

◆ *Step 1*. Begin by making a list of the areas to be agreed upon or questions you need answers to, using the material discussed earlier in this chapter. You might want to create a chart or just itemize areas on a notepad. You will need to write down areas such as Communications (see page 30 for a suggested list of questions), Progress Reports, Working Pattern (again, some suggested questions are discussed on page 33), and Level of Proactivity. Next to each item, you can make your own notes when you find the answers. Allow yourself a three-month period to get all the answers.

◆ *Step 2*. Start trying to fill in your chart or finding answers to your questions by asking or observing. Some things will be appropriate to take up with your boss, but for others you could try asking colleagues who have been there longer or know your boss better. Other issues will be resolved simply by seeing how your boss behaves and inferring what she expects from that.

◆ *Step 3*. Constantly review your psychological contract once you have completed it. Expectations change, especially in today's turbulent business climate. New staff, new technology, and new patterns of working can all mean your psychological contract will need reviewing.

SUMMARY

In this chapter we have looked at the main areas that should be considered when establishing a psychological contract with your boss. Such an unwritten contract is important because it allows you to meet your boss's expectations and thus ensure that she is happy with you. Making your boss happy is, after all, the key to good boss management! Once you have established your psychological contract, you can use it to really impress your boss and this is what we will concentrate on in the following chapter.

Chapter 4

How to Impress
Your Boss

Perhaps the most important aspect to really managing your boss lies in your willingness and ability to impress him. The boss who is impressed by you is likely to think highly of you and therefore reward you in a range of ways, from praise to promotion. By impressing your boss, you are thus influencing or managing your own prospects. In this chapter we will examine the ways you can start impressing your boss from day one, by creating that all-important good first impression, and right through your working life with a commitment to professionalism. Issues covered here include

1. creating a good first impression.

2. body language.

3. emotion management.

4. professionalism.

CREATING A GOOD FIRST IMPRESSION

First impressions are everything. Humans tend to make snap judgments about people, events, and things, simply because we do not have enough time to invest in careful consideration before reaching a decision. And the decision we make about whether someone or something is good or bad can be long-lasting and difficult to shake off. This means that if your initial encounter with the boss is negative, you will need to invest a great deal of energy into reversing

that impression; moreover, everything you do will be tarnished with that negative impression. On the other hand, a great first impression means that you are blessed with a head start and everything else you do will seem that much better, thanks to that good first impression. Psychologists refer to this as the "horns or halo effect." You therefore need to make sure the effect you create is a halo, which helps ensure that everything else you do is perceived in a more positive light, rather than horns, which makes everything else you do appear more negative.

You can start creating a halo effect from the very first introduction or meeting with your boss. Follow the guidelines, on page 44.

BODY LANGUAGE

What you say to the boss is sometimes less important than how you say it, and the tone conveyed by your body language can betray your true feelings. On the other hand, being aware of your body language and making it work for you can make the difference between impressing your boss and leaving him

Guidelines for creating a halo effect at the first meeting with the boss

Handshake	Offer a firm handshake with a smile; this conveys self-confidence and interest. Shake your boss's hand no more—or less—than three times so as not to create the impression that you are nervous. Beware of turning your hand down over his since this can create an impression of the desire for dominance. Similarly, don't offer an overfamiliar handshake—involving two hands, grasping your boss's wrist, elbow, or shoulder, and so on.
Introduction	If appropriate, introduce yourself in a clear, nonapologetic voice. Remember to smile and maintain eye contact.
Small talk	Now that the introduction is over, make sure that you don't just stand there looking awkward. Make small talk: Comment on the weather (always a good one), your trip there, the building. Try to make a positive rather than negative comment to create the impression that you are upbeat and optimistic.
Questions	Ask your boss general questions, nothing too personal or that requires too lengthy or detailed a response. Look interested in his response.
Interest	Demonstrate that you are hugely interested in your boss's every word by gazing intently at him, remembering to look away at times too (see page 43 for discussion on body language) and making the occasional affirmative sound such as "Uh-huh."
Dress	See page 52 for dress codes.
Body language	See the charts on pages 45 and 46 for specifics about body language in two types of circumstances—in meetings and in the office in general.

with a decidedly negative impression of you. There are two main situations in which you can really use your body language to impress: in meetings and generally in the office. Use the pointers in the charts on this and the next page as a guide.

EMOTION MANAGEMENT

Few people understand what is meant by emotion management, much less use it to impress their boss. Yet it is probably one of the

IN MEETINGS

Do . . .	Don't . . .
have a pen in your hand. A poised pen creates the impression that you are ready for action, attentive, and interested.	play with the pen or tap it on the desk as this just creates the impression that you are bored.
make occasional notes. Again, this really shows you are interested in the proceedings.	doodle; it will probably be noticed and nothing conveys boredom more!
sit slightly forward in your chair. This makes you appear to be hanging onto every word and waiting for the right moment to add your own contribution.	lean back with your hands behind your head. This might be a comfortable position but can make you seem arrogant and overconfident, as if the proceedings of the meeting are somewhat beneath you.
keep hands still. Too much fluttering and movement conveys the impression that your mind is wandering with your hands.	constantly touch your hair or mouth, or pick imaginary bits of fluff off your clothes. This can make you appear, at worst, shifty, and at best, uninterested.

IN THE OFFICE

Do . . .	Don't . . .
use "open" body language such as uncrossed arms and legs. This creates the impression that you have nothing to hide and that you are reasonably confident.	constantly sit with your legs and arms crossed as this can make you appear secretive and defensive to your boss. It is OK to cross your legs as long as you keep your arms open. Similarly, beware of standing with your hands on your hips or waist in an aggressive stance.
try to maintain a relaxed stance, even if you have to work at it. It might feel unnatural at first, but try putting one hand in your pocket as you move around, or lean on a desk slightly as you talk to your boss. This conveys confidence.	hold yourself as if you are a soldier at attention. This can make you seem stiff and formal as well as unsure about yourself, not the impression you want to leave with your boss.
keep your distance. Personal body space is important, so when you are talking to your boss (or anyone else), make sure you are not too close; if he is constantly edging away from you, then you are too close.	invade your boss's personal space, nor should you stand too far away, as that can make you seem cold and distant. Try to follow his lead.
try mirroring your boss's body language. If he inclines his head slightly, you do it too. This creates a responsive impression, subtly suggesting that you are in tune with him.	overdo the mirroring; directly copying every body movement can be downright embarrassing and counterproductive.

most influential and ongoing acts of impression management that you could undertake. Emotion management refers to the deliberate attempt to control the emotions that you present to other people. Most of us perform emotion management at some point in our working—and nonworking—lives, for example,

◆ when we laugh at our boss's (unfunny) joke.

◆ when we express sympathy at our colleague's bad news, even if we don't really care.

◆ when we fake enthusiasm about the achievements of our friends' children.

◆ when we hide our annoyance at an irritating customer.

These are all examples of emotion management—almost unconscious acts that form an important part of all our social interactions. By controlling and managing the emotional front we present to others, we help make interactions run more smoothly, we make people feel good about themselves, and we help ensure that the impression we create of ourselves is the one we want others to perceive. Imagine how unpopular we would be if we never engaged in any emotion management! The following three-step guide should help you use emotion management to impress your boss.

Step 1: Recognize the emotions that will impress your boss
Using emotion management to impress your boss is just taking what we all do naturally one step further. The first step is to recognize and acknowledge the emotions that will impress your boss. It is worth noting that research in the area suggests that two kinds of emotional display are best avoided in the workplace.

These are

1. negative emotions, such as anger, disappointment, jealousy.

2. extreme displays of emotion, such as crying, temper tantrums, inappropriate joy.

So, at the very least, make sure you control your emotions and avoid these displays. This means that even if your boss has really annoyed you, or you have won the lottery—assuming it's not such a big win that you can quit your job—you should still think carefully about the emotional front you are presenting. Of course, this means that, invariably, you will have to suppress or hide your true feelings at times. Some people feel this is unnecessary and have a kind of WYSIWYG attitude—"what you see is what you get." Fair enough, but this won't impress the boss.

So, those are the emotions that won't impress your boss, but what emotions will? Research has shown that most bosses and managers tend to be more impressed by displays of enthusiasm or interest than anything else. Showing enthusiasm demonstrates to your boss that you are eager, hardworking, and loyal, and that you care about the company, are passionate about your work, and are ambitious. All that from just a simple act of emotion management!

Of course, it is not just one simple act of emotion management that is needed; to be truly effective, emotion management needs to be an ongoing activity. Display enthusiasm and interest by

◆ smiling when you see your boss or when you are assigned tasks or projects.

◆ rising to the challenge of a new assignment instead of appearing not to want to do it.

◆ being positive about ideas and projects, not negative.

◆ volunteering for jobs.

◆ asking appropriate questions.

You should be careful, however, of two points.

1. Avoid going over the top with your emotional displays. Enthusiasm and interest may well be valued, but constant grinning at your boss every time you see him, boundless enthusiasm for even the most inappropriate tasks, and constantly leaping up to volunteer for jobs will not endear you to your coworkers—or to your boss. In fact, your boss is more likely to view you as an ingratiating irritant!

2. Avoid reserving your displays of enthusiasm just for your boss's benefit. Switching it on and off will make you appear false rather than enthusiastic and interested. The trick to appearing enthusiastic is to actually *be* enthusiastic. This way there is nothing phony or superficial about you, nor can you be accused of being manipulative. The next step provides tips on creating enthusiasm even when you don't actually feel it.

Step 2: Learn how to fake and hide
It is inevitable that the emotions you ought to display in order to impress your boss will not necessarily be those that you genuinely feel. You will, at times, be obliged to display enthusiasm when you do not feel remotely enthusiastic, or hide anger when you feel it. Consider the following scenarios.

◆ You are preoccupied by a personal worry or concern.

◆ You are distressed by an argument with your partner.

◆ You have a health worry.

◆ You have been passed over for promotion.

◆ Your colleague is assigned a task that should have gone to you.

◆ A customer is manipulating you.

◆ Your boss wants your opinion on a project that doesn't interest you.

◆ Your car broke down and you are late for a meeting.

◆ A customer has just been rude to you.

◆ You feel ill.

These are common situations that occur at work on a day-to-day basis that make it very difficult to display the required emotions while simultaneously hiding your real ones. Yet, if you are to impress and ultimately manage your boss, you must fake and hide.

There are two approaches to this emotional acting and both have their roots in schools of professional acting.

◆ *Surface acting.* Professional actors know this as technical acting and it involves simply arranging your physical features so that they reflect the emotion you want to display. That is, in this approach, there is no need to try to feel the required emotion at all. However, the act of arranging your facial features in, for example, a smile could in itself induce the associated feeling of happiness because it is thought that the very act of smiling causes physiological and chemical changes in our brain, making us *feel* happy.

◆ *Deep acting.* This is known by professional actors as the method approach and involves the actor attempting to conjure up the emotion that he is required to display. In other words, in this approach, you would actually try to feel enthusiastic. The founder of method acting, Stanislavski, advised that this can be achieved by using a technique called emotional memory, which involves you recalling an experience or incident when you *did* feel the required emotion in the past, and using that memory to help you feel that emotion now.

Both these approaches are fine if you must do an occasional bit of acting. For instance, our research has shown that most of us hide or fake emotion in about a third of our workplace communications and doing so allows us to impress the boss so that we can get ahead at work. However, if you find that you are constantly hiding and faking emotion, then it is time for a reassessment. Perhaps you never feel enthusiastic about work, or dislike your boss. It is difficult under those circumstances to manage your boss without addressing the root cause of your work-based dissatisfaction. The common problems covered in Chapter 7 might help.

Step 3: Diagnosing the emotional culture at work
In addition to ensuring that you display emotions such as enthusiasm and interest discussed in Steps 1 and 2, as a good emotion and impression manager you will go one step further if you really want to manage your boss. You will diagnose the *emotional culture* of your organization or company so that you can be sure that your own emotional demeanor matches it. The emotional culture of the organization refers to the unwritten rules about which emotions

should be displayed and which should be hidden; these are not the same for every company or industry. More creative industries allow freer emotional expression and it may even be appropriate in some to display the extreme emotional displays that are frowned upon in other office cultures. On the other hand, some emotional cultures are such that no emotions are expected at all—not even enthusiasm.

PROFESSIONALISM

What does it mean to be professional? Being professional is the difference between doing your job adequately and doing it well enough to justify not only your salary, but a possible increase too. Professionalism is about attention to detail, showing you care about your work, and not letting anyone (including yourself) down. Professionalism is about proving to your boss that you are more than capable, which is why it is a key aspect of managing your boss; if your boss trusts you and relies on you, he will be more likely to reward you with extra responsibilities, perks, training, and so on. Achieve professionalism by careful attention to the following areas.

PERSONAL APPEARANCE

In general, you should aim to ensure that your personal appearance sets you apart from a student on an internship. This means neat hair, pressed clothing, and an emphasis on classic rather than trendy attire. Go easy on fussy details such as jewelry and over-powering scents. The impression you should be trying to create is that you are hardworking and not preoccupied or distracted by your appearance. In addition, you want your boss to be confident that you are presentable to clients and customers, even if they should arrive unexpectedly.

Of course, what you wear depends on the dress code of your office and, like emotional culture discussed earlier, this can vary between industries and organizations. It might be more acceptable in such creative fields as the arts or the media to wear casual attire, but less so in most other industries. The best way of ensuring that you look as professional as you can is to dress in a style similar to your boss; dress for the job you want, not the job you have.

TIME MANAGEMENT

Perfecting your time-management skills is a vital step to appearing professional. If you have good time-management skills, you should have few problems in

◆ submitting reports on time.

◆ meeting deadlines.

◆ being able to update your boss on progress whenever it is requested.

◆ being punctual for meetings.

◆ arriving at work on time.

◆ being able to give accurate estimates about how long work projects will take you.

All these are signs of professionalism. Improve your time-management skills by

◆ learning to prioritize work so that you complete the most urgent or important tasks first rather than the ones you *want* to do first.

◆ delegating where possible.

◆ discouraging interruptions; a huge amount of time is wasted through interruptions from colleagues and phone calls. If you are completing a job for a deadline, either build interruption time into your estimate of how long it will take you, or put your voice mail on and a Please Do Not Disturb sign on your office door.

◆ being organized in your filing and storage systems.

◆ keeping checklists so that you know exactly what needs doing and you don't end up forgetting anything.

◆ being realistic so that when you estimate how long a job will take, you do not underestimate. Similarly, make sure you do not take on tasks that you will not have time to complete.

YOUR DESK

Your desk can make or break your impression as a professional. Create a professional image by

◆ keeping your desk free of clutter.

◆ having an In box system that shows a good volume of Out work completed.

◆ keeping personal possessions such as photographs to a minimum.

◆ choosing decorative items with care—potted plants are fine, but avoid silly computer mats or novelty pens.

PRESENTATION OF WORK

The appearance of your work is an indicator of your professionalism. It is not enough for it just to be delivered on time or even to be

of superior quality; it must look professional too. This allows the way your work is presented to act as a halo so that the good impression created is seen in the content, too (see pages 42–43 for notes on the halo effect). Create a professional image in your work by

◆ ensuring accuracy—check and double-check.

◆ avoiding spelling, grammatical, and typing errors.

◆ binding reports in suitable covers.

◆ using appropriate color in reports or presentations.

SUMMARY

In this chapter we have concentrated on impressing your boss so that he will be more likely to reward you with a promotion, pay raises, perks, or extra responsibilities—that is what managing your boss is all about. You can concentrate on first impressions, your body language, emotion management, and professionalism to impress your boss. In the following chapter we will turn our attention to getting more from your boss, such as how to ask for a raise or more challenging work.

Chapter 5

Getting More from Your Boss

By now you should be well on your way to successfully managing your boss, but to really get ahead at work you will need to know how to get even more from your boss. It is a rare employee who is totally happy with the conditions and workload her boss offers; most of us will, at some point, need to ask or negotiate for more. Yet doing so is something that many people find extremely difficult and the result is that they are burdened with too much work, boring tasks, or poor pay, or are overlooked for promotion for far too long. In this chapter, we will focus on approaching some of the more common areas that need to be addressed in order to get more from your boss. These include

1. asking for a raise.

2. seeking promotion.

3. requesting more challenging work.

4. dealing with work overload.

Before tackling these issues, it is worth addressing the question of why so many people are unable to ask for what they want from their boss. Common reasons for people accepting rather than challenging the status quo include:

I don't want to rock the boat.

I don't want my boss to think that I am not dedicated enough by complaining about my work hours.

My boss likes enthusiastic workers; I will seem like a whiner if I complain.

I should be able to cope, shouldn't I? If I ask for a reduction in my workload, I will seem less capable.

I can't ask for a raise because if my boss hasn't already given me one, maybe she doesn't think I deserve it.

Maybe I am not good enough for promotion.

All these sentiments reflect a lack of self-confidence and a failure to recognize basic work rights. The trick, therefore, to getting more from your boss is to become more assertive at work.

BECOMING MORE ASSERTIVE AT WORK

The first step to becoming more assertive is to recognize and accept the work-related rights that you, as an employee, have. These include

◆ the right to be fairly paid for the work you do.

◆ the right to perform tasks that you are qualified to do—and not to perform tasks for which you are not qualified.

◆ the right to enjoy a life outside of work.

◆ the right to equality of opportunity.

◆ the right to not be threatened, abused, or otherwise harassed at work.

◆ the right to say No to inappropriate requests at work.

◆ the right to work under conditions that are not detrimental to your physical or mental health.

In addition to these basic moral rights, every full-time employee also has legal rights. These include

◆ the right to not be unfairly dismissed.

◆ the right to return to your job after maternity leave.

◆ the right to not be discriminated against because of disability, sex, or race.

◆ the right to have time off for postnatal care.

◆ the right to (unpaid) time off for jury duty and for union activities.

◆ the right to time off in the event of downsizing to look for work or arrange for training.

◆ the right to a written statement of the reason for dismissal.

◆ the right to have itemized pay statements.

◆ the right to not have the employment contract breached.

◆ the right to be paid the minimum wage.

If you are able to accept that you have these rights—as do all your coworkers and, indeed, your boss—then you are on the way to being able to assert them. Much of the reticence that workers have in asking for more from their boss is tied up with their being unsure of their basic rights. Thus, if you can accept that you have the right to a life outside of work, for instance, then it is easier to give yourself permission to complain about being expected to work on weekends. Similarly, if you believe that you are entitled to work under conditions that are not going to have pernicious effects on your health, you should feel more comfortable about challenging a work environment that is particularly stressful.

Of course, it's one thing to realize that it is perfectly acceptable to ask your boss for more, but it's quite another to actually do it! The rest of this chapter will help.

ASKING FOR A RAISE

Before you even think about how to go about asking for a raise, stop and ask yourself one crucial question: Do I deserve a raise? That might seem like a strange question, but many people make the mistake of seeking a raise for the wrong reasons. Here are some of them.

◆ My coworker was given a raise so I should get one too.

◆ I have been with the firm a long time.

◆ My friend who works for company X earns more than I do.

◆ I have just had a baby; I need more money.

None of these reasons has anything to do with the value you offer the company and therefore they are irrelevant when it comes to seeking a raise. Legitimate reasons (over and above normal inflationary increases) include the following:

♦ I have been given more responsibility at work and should be paid accordingly.

♦ I am working longer hours because there is more work to do—not because I am a slow worker.

♦ I have saved the company money, for example, with a cost-cutting idea.

♦ I am expected to work longer hours.

♦ I am expected to travel or be away from home more.

♦ I have gained relevant new skills or qualifications, which mean I am adding more value to the company.

Once you have established that you have a good case, your next task is figuring out how to manage your boss so that she agrees. The best strategy is to present a logical, coherent argument, either as a written report or a verbal presentation. Either way, you will need to arrange a meeting with your boss. If there is an evaluation system in place in your company, a good time to do this is at that point; if there is no evaluation system, you might like to suggest one for yourself—it is just an annual review of your strengths and weaknesses so that training needs, promotion prospects, and so on can be identified.

When you meet with your boss, using the following pointers as guidelines to help you have a successful outcome.

1. *Don't threaten.* It is common for workers to make the mistake of saying such things as, "If I don't get a pay raise, I will be forced to look for alternative employment." Don't make such threats unless you fully intend to follow them through, and only if you actually have a job to go to! Many bosses will be irritated by such threats and may well take you up on your offer.

2. *Don't demand.* You have every right to request a pay raise, but you cannot demand one. Nothing will annoy your boss more than feeling that her hand is forced.

3. *Stay calm.* It is normal to feel quite emotional about the request; after all, your livelihood is at stake. Staying calm and reasonable will help—becoming petulant or emotional will not.

Of course, there is still every possibility that the boss may say No, however well reasoned your argument might be. It could be that your boss does not think you deserve one after all, or that the company simply cannot afford any more money. In the former case, it is worth finding out what more you could do to become more deserving. In the latter case, ask for a review in, say, six months. In both cases, this should ensure that No is not the final answer.

Another common excuse that some bosses give for turning down a request for a raise is that "If I give you one I will have to give one to your coworkers." This is an unacceptable reason and you will have to make it clear that you are representing yourself only and that you do not and will not discuss your salary with anyone else.

SEEKING PROMOTION
Many of the issues regarding promotion are similar to those concerned with asking for a pay raise. However, seeking promotion involves some extra considerations. There are two main scenarios.

1. There is a specific vacancy that you wish to be promoted to.

2. There is no specific vacancy; you just want to move up the ladder.

Both of these scenarios require different approaches to the boss. Where there is a *specific vacancy*, for instance when a more senior person has left the firm, leaving that position vacant, you will have to persuade your boss not only that you are suitable for the higher position, but that you are more suitable than anyone else. It is increasingly common for any vacancy to be advertised externally, so you may be competing against an unknown entity, too.

The first step is to approach your boss to stake your claim. Follow these guidelines:

◆ As soon as the vacancy becomes apparent (this could be before the other person has left), meet with your boss and explain why you think you would be the best person for the job.

◆ Include in your argument any evidence to show that you could do the job well and remember to point out why you want the job so much.

◆ Whatever you do, avoid criticizing the previous holder of the position. If you have some ideas on changes or improvements you would make, present them in a way that does not appear critical of your hoped-for predecessor.

At this point, it is likely that you will receive some feedback regarding your application. Hopefully, it will be of the positive, go-for-it kind. You may be invited or advised to put in a written application or to apply along the same route as everyone else. Because this is the likely outcome, some people make the mistake of bypassing the boss completely and jumping right to the application stage. Since your boss is sure to be asked about your suitability, it is eminently sensible to gain her approval first—she is far more likely to recommend you if she has been consulted in advance.

But what if the feedback from your boss is less than positive? Find out the reason; then you can do something about it, if necessary. Perhaps your boss does not think you are ready for the responsibility or thinks you lack some necessary skill or experience. Whatever it is that she thinks is missing from your résumé, now is your chance to ask for the training or tasks that will fill the gap. If you consider your boss's assessment of you to be fair, it is wise not to go ahead with the application for promotion.

But suppose you consider your boss's comments to be unfair or untrue? Suppose they claim that you have not demonstrated managerial skills, yet you know you ran the office effectively for one month while your superior was out sick? The trick here is to tact-

fully point this out, without actually appearing to say to your boss, "You are SO wrong!" Ask whether she is aware of the positive feedback you received while managing the office for that month and explain how much you enjoyed the challenge and feel ready for more. If you are totally unable to convince your boss, it might be worth trying to convince someone else from a different company— in other words, look for another job at the level you want. However, you should bear in mind that your current boss is likely to be asked for a reference.

So why might your boss refuse to refer you for promotion, even when you seem to have the right skills and experience? Of course, it is always possible that she is right and you are overplaying your abilities. On the other hand, there are rare circumstances when a boss might deliberately hold you back, either because she doesn't want to lose you or because she feels threatened by you. Both these scenarios are difficult to overcome and if you suspect this is happening to you, it really could be time to jump ship—see if there is anyone else in the firm who could give you a reference.

When there is no *specific vacancy*, much of the above will still apply, but you are in a slightly better position in that you don't have to wait for someone else to leave. A good time to suggest a promotion is at your annual review or when you have just gained some relevant skill or qualification. Again, if the answer is No, find out what you will need to do to get a Yes next time. And make sure you do it.

REQUESTING MORE CHALLENGING WORK
Many people remain stuck for years with entry-level tasks simply because they are waiting for their boss to give them more rewarding work. Don't wait! Asking for more challenging work demon-

strates enthusiasm and eagerness, and most bosses like that. The best advice here, therefore, is to be proactive and always be on the lookout for more interesting jobs that you could offer to do. Suggest work that you could take on, either tasks that would save your boss from doing them, ideas that you have come up with, or work that no one else in the office wants. Here are a few top tips.

◆ To show your ability, actually do something (even if it is only a mockup) and show it to your boss.

◆ If you want to learn a new skill that might get you more rewarding work, shadow or closely observe a more experienced colleague.

◆ Request training so that you will be able to take on more interesting work.

◆ Spend time with the people whose jobs you aspire to; you can learn a lot from them over informal chats at lunch.

◆ Always ask to do specific work; don't just vaguely complain that the work is "not challenging enough."

◆ Be realistic—don't run before you can walk. There is no point asking to edit a newsletter, for instance, if you have never even written an article for it.

DEALING WITH WORK OVERLOAD
Many readers may have turned to this section first; having too much work to do is a very common problem. But what is too much? You know you are suffering from work overload if

1. you are continually having to work late.

2. you have to take work home with you.

3. you always feel pressured and stressed.

4. you never have time for lunch.

Work overload is potentially quite a serious issue because it is a significant source of stress in the workplace. And stress itself can lead to a lowered immunity, which is why you are likely to suffer from repeated colds, flu, and other ailments. Remember your rights, and take action. Arrange a meeting with your boss and present her with a time sheet in which you have listed your work tasks and time required to complete them over the past month. This should demonstrate clearly that you have too much work. Explain that you are happy for occasional heavy workloads, for instance, when deadlines are approaching or a heavy order needs filling, but that you cannot continue this way indefinitely.

If you can suggest solutions to the problem, all the better, since it will always impress people if you appear to have the company's interests at heart as well as your own. For instance, there may be areas of your job that could be cut or delegated to someone else. There may be some tasks that could be shortened in terms of cutting corners. Of course, it may be that there simply needs to be more staff—not usually a welcome suggestion in these cost-cutting days.

The final word of this chapter has to be: Don't put up with chronic work overload. Your health could well suffer, so if your boss is not forthcoming with help, then think about moving on.

SUMMARY

In this chapter we have learned how to get more from your boss in four main areas—getting a pay raise or promotion, requesting more challenging work, and reducing work overload. All these involve knowing your basic work rights and being able to assert them. In the next chapter we will consider those situations where it seems impossible to get more from your boss—when you have the boss from hell!

Chapter 6

Dealing with the Boss from Hell

Everything discussed so far is all well and good if you have a boss who is a fairly reasonable human being. But what happens if you have a boss who won't listen to reason, who is motivated by selfish desires, who is abusive and arrogant—who, in other words, is the boss from hell? Such a boss is unlikely to be managed through normal means such as a psychological contract (see Chapter 3) or impression management (Chapter 4). If you have a boss from hell, you might need to take more dramatic action if you are to even begin to manage him and the distress that his behavior causes you.

In this chapter we will discuss how to deal with the three worst types of bosses from hell:

---

1. the bullying boss

2. the sexually harassing boss

3. the glory-stealing boss

THE BULLYING BOSS

Is your boss a bully?

Before we talk about how to deal with the boss who is bullying you, we need to define what we mean by a bullying boss. When

does a bad-tempered, rude boss become a bully? One researcher defines such bullying as "persistent criticism and personal abuse, both in public and in private, which humiliates and demeans the individual, gradually eroding his sense of self," while others have stated that bullying at work is "persistent, offensive, abusive, intimidating, malicious, or insulting behavior, abuse of power, or unfair penal sanctions, which make the recipient feel upset, threatened, humiliated, or vulnerable, and which undermines his self-confidence and may cause him to suffer stress." As a general guide, your boss may be a bully if he

◆ explodes angrily, either in an indiscriminate way or in a focused manner.

◆ picks on you (or/and others) unfairly.

◆ humiliates you in front of others.

◆ pressures you into doing things you don't want to do or doing things his way.

- forces you to abandon your own plans, such as by making you work late against your will.

- asserts his power over you—he can fire you if you don't do what he wants you to do.

- constantly criticizes you.

- ridicules you.

- belittles your achievements.

- unreasonably refuses your requests.

- sets unrealistic deadlines.

- shouts at you (or others).

Care should be taken when trying to decide if your boss could be classified as a bully. He does not need to display all of these behaviors, but the point is that his behavior is continually abusive rather than a one-time only event. Your boss is not a bully if his complaints about you are focused and justified, although shouting and ridiculing are never justified.

IS IT SERIOUS?

If you do indeed think that your boss might be a bully, then, yes, it is a very serious matter. Some people have the view that bullying bosses are par for the course, a result of the everyday pressures and strains of work. Bosses, they argue, do not have time for common niceties—they must shout and cajole to get things done. But, there is a clear difference between an impatient or stressed boss and the bullying one. You will probably know if your boss is a bully without having to go through the previous checklist. Research shows that workplace bullying can lead to serious health problems for the employee and you may already be experiencing one or more of the following:

◆ Feelings of high stress

◆ Repeated colds and minor infections

◆ Depression or other mental health problems

◆ Inability to perform your job

◆ Dread of work

In fact, workplace bullying is now taken very seriously. It is already being recognized as a significant factor contributing to workplace stress, with potentially substantial costs for both individuals and for industry. According to a recent survey, a quarter of adult workers have been subjected to bullying at some point in their working lives, while another study suggests that many working days are lost each year due to the effects of bullying in the workplace.

WHY IS YOUR BOSS A BULLY?

Psychologists and researchers have invested a great deal of energy into trying to find out why people bully other people. Several theories emerge, including

1. *The childhood pay-off theory.* It has been said that to understand why adults bully, it is first necessary to understand that many of them discovered in childhood that bullying can have positive results. For some, bullying may be a way of attempting to come to terms with abuse suffered as a child. For others, their behavior may be an attempt to win love or attention from their parents, reflecting parental neglect. This bully, therefore, is likely

to be a bully even if he is not a boss. He does not use bullying as a means of managing, but as a general way to get what he wants.

2. *The envy/threat theory*. Others argue that envy is a major motivator for bullying behavior; a bully boss may attack certain individuals for various reasons, the most common being the victim's popularity among colleagues, success, achievement, efficiency, organizational expertise, and superior social skills. This boss feels threatened by the up-and-coming subordinate who may seem to be better at the job than he is and may eventually usurp him. This boss is insecure and lacks confidence in his own abilities and is more likely to bully only one or two people rather than a larger group.

3. *The personality theory*. Many researchers argue that bullies have certain personality or behavioral characteristics. For instance, researchers claim that there are four types of bully bosses ranging from the pathological bully who bullies for enjoyment, the situational bully who resorts to bullying when under pressure, the role-playing bully who feels that bullying behavior is expected of him, and the punishing bully who believes that punishment is an effective means of management. They have found that many people bully because they have employees on their staff whom they find difficult and they do not know how else to manage them; they bully as a means of passing on their own stress, or because they work in environments where this is the norm and they can simply get away with it.

MANAGING THE BULLY BOSS

There are a range of strategies that the victim of a bully boss can adopt. Here are some of them.

Knowing your rights

In the previous chapter we looked at workers' rights, and it is important to revisit and remember these if your boss is a bully; often, bullying behavior will infringe upon these rights. In addition to the rights that every worker is entitled to, there are legal rights that are relevant to the bully boss. Although you have no legal right not to be bullied at work, if your boss's bullying causes you to leave your job, become ill, or is based on sexual or racial harassment (see Chapter 7), then you may have cause to take legal action. In addition, there is the criminal offense of intentional harassment, which could apply to the bully boss if he threatens or insults you. Other laws exist that may well be weapons against the bully boss if such behavior means that the worker's rights to be treated humanely are violated. You will need to seek legal advice in order to implement any of these acts, but this should be considered only if all else has failed.

Confrontation

Knowing your rights is one thing, but being able to assert them is something else. Being assertive with a bully boss means calmly pointing out that you dislike his behavior and find it unacceptable—in other words, confronting your boss. The best way to confront a bully boss is probably not in a reactive way, that is, not when he has just bullied you. Such a confrontation is likely to be aggressive, either on your or the bully's part, and counterproductive. To confront your bully boss effectively, you need to arrange a meeting with him and explain your concerns. Explain that you feel victimized, or that you feel pressured to do things, or that your rights are infringed. Be polite and calm—but not apologetic. You could even ask why the bully is behaving that way; it is always possible that your boss has no idea about the distress he is causing you, especially if he feels that bullying is a normal and effective management tool. If confrontation fails, you may need to try the next strategy.

Making an official complaint

To do this, you will need to gather evidence of your bully boss's behavior. Keep a diary of any incidents that caused you distress. Note what happened and when. Mention any witnesses to the incident, as well as how it made you feel. Now you are ready to complain.

The first thing to do is to find out if your company has a policy regarding workplace bullying. Some do, although this is not yet a legal requirement. If there is one, you can follow those guidelines; otherwise, you will have to follow a formal grievances procedure— ask your human resources department if you are not sure about this.

If your company is a smaller one without such procedures, then make a complaint in writing to your boss's manager or superior. Explain in the letter that you have evidence and witnesses and that you would like action taken.

If a formal complaint does not halt the bully boss in his tracks, you may have to consider taking legal action.

Taking legal action

This should always be considered a last resort since it is costly and time consuming, and usually means you will have to leave your job in order to pursue the case. By this stage, you should have amassed a good portfolio of evidence and probably medical evidence too— visits to your doctor with stress-related problems can be used as evidence. Approach your union advisor or a lawyer for advice on how to proceed (and see the next section on sexual harassment).

THE SEXUALLY HARASSING BOSS

Sexual harassment occurs when your boss (or any other person, of course) offers unwanted conduct that affects your dignity in the workplace. The key is that the actions or comments are viewed as demeaning and unacceptable to the recipient.

Harassment, which can be by male or female bosses toward male or female subordinates, can be an isolated incident but is usually persistent. Generally, sexual harassment could involve

◆ unwelcome sexual advances such as touching.

◆ standing too close.

◆ sexual comments.

◆ a display of offensive materials.

◆ questions of a sexual nature.

◆ personal comments regarding physical attributes.

Your boss does not need to do any of this face to face; sexual harassment can also occur in written communications, e-mail, or by phone.

IS IT SERIOUS?

As with bullying, sexual harassment can have serious effects on the health and well-being of employees. Victims may feel

◆ anxious.

◆ humiliated.

◆ frightened.

- ◆ angry.

- ◆ frustrated.

- ◆ unable to cope.

- ◆ unwilling to go to work.

- ◆ demotivated.

- ◆ unwell.

- ◆ stressed.

All these commonly experienced symptoms can, of course, lead to reduced work performance, absence from work, and even resignation. Employers do have a legal responsibility to protect your health, safety, and welfare, but if it is your boss doing the harassing, what can you do? Use the following as a guide.

Confrontation

The first step is to let your boss know that his actions are causing you distress. He genuinely may not mean to harass you and may think he is just being flirty or cute. Some people are more touchy-feely than others and may not realize how offensive this touching is. By telling him, you are giving him a chance to stop, which he will do if it was unintended. Even if he is aware that his behavior is inappropriate, by confronting him, you can make him see that you are aware of your rights and will not accept his behavior; in many cases this is enough to stop him. Be firm, not aggressive, and be positive and calm, but not apologetic. The following would be a reasonable approach:

> *You might not realize it but when you put your arm around me in the office/tell off-color jokes, I feel very uncomfortable and I would like you to stop doing this.*

If you find it too difficult to confront your boss face to face, try sending an e-mail or memo—keep a copy and any reply.

Keep a diary

As with the bullying boss, you are advised to make a note of any incidents that you believe are evidence that your boss is sexually harassing you. Record the dates, times, any witnesses, and how you felt at the time. Keep copies of any relevant evidence such as letters, memos, tapes, e-mails, etc. Keep records of any medical help you seek, such as treatment for stress or depression.

Seek advice

Talk to your union representative or human resources department. These sources may be able to advise you on how to proceed and what action to take—and whether or not you have a case for legal action.

Formal complaint

This procedure would be similar to that used when dealing with the bully boss (see page 78).

Legal recourse

As with the bullying situation, you will usually be able to assert your legal rights only if you leave the company, although claims alleging sex discrimination can be made while you are still employed. If you do take legal action, it will probably involve filing a lawsuit, and the court will expect you to have made every effort to first resolve the problem yourself.

EMPLOYEES' RIGHTS

Knowing your rights under the law can be helpful in dealing with both a bully and a sexually harrassing boss. For information regarding federal laws and regulations and their enforcement, you may visit the web site of the U.S. Equal Employment Opportunity Commission:

www.eeoc.gov

or phone that office at (800) 669-4000, TDD (800) 669-6820.

THE GLORY-STEALING BOSS
The glory-stealing boss is the one who

◆ passes off your ideas as his own.

◆ criticizes your ideas but reworks them as his own.

◆ claims responsibility for your successes, but not your failures.

◆ does not give you credit for good work.

Such a boss may not seem quite as hellish as the bullying or harassing boss and, certainly, there are unlikely to be avenues of legal redress to turn to, but the glory-stealing boss can still make your

work life very difficult and can even block promotions and career progression. After all, if no one knows how well you are doing, how will you ever get promoted? And, when it comes to downsizing, you could be first in line if your skills and talent are not filtering out beyond your department to the powers that be.

A good boss will always credit you with good work, and tell others about you. After all, it reflects well on him if his staff is performing well. However, to an insecure boss, the fear is that you will outperform him, which is why he may feel the need to claim the credit and keep you in your place.

IS YOUR BOSS STEALING YOUR GLORY?

It can take a while before you find out that your glory is being stolen, especially if your boss creates the impression that he has been singing your praises to everyone. It might be several months— or even years—down the line before you find out that your boss never mentions you at those board meetings. So, the first step toward dealing with this kind of boss from hell is to find out if there is a problem at all. Here are clues you should be looking for.

◆ Ideas that your boss has said will "never work" later appear in memos or reports that he has produced.

◆ Your boss encourages you to put his name as coauthor on any report you prepare.

◆ When you speak to people from other departments they know nothing of your successes.

◆ When you meet senior management they barely seem to know who you are.

◆ Your boss insists that personal glory detracts from team effort, and therefore your name is left out of reports detailing the "department's" successes.

◆ Your boss encourages all upward communications to go through him.

BEATING THE GLORY-STEALING BOSS

The glory-stealing boss can be beaten, but it takes some effort. Once you are fairly sure that your boss is either stealing your credit or blocking your glory from reaching beyond the department, it is time to take action. The next time you have a major success, such as a great idea, a money-saving strategy, and so on, follow this boss-management plan.

Keep records

Keep records of any memos or conversations you have with your boss so that you can prove that those great ideas have indeed been initiated by you and not by your boss. Keep copies of replies from your boss and encourage written ones by e-mailing or memoing queries, such as, "Have you had a chance to look over my idea yet?" rather than face to face or on the phone.

Get the evidence

It is always a good idea to obtain some piece of external evidence to back up your brilliance; otherwise it is easy for your boss to belittle your achievement. Evidence can include a letter from a customer, statistical reports documenting savings, an original (dated) memo outlining a proposal, and the like.

Bypass your boss

There's no easy way around this—your boss cannot be trusted to spread the word so you will need to do it yourself. Your method of (self) publicity depends on what it is you want to tell the world. A memo to the head office or to the executive board might be best if there is something really outstanding to report, but remember to mention your boss in a positive way to deflect the inevitable unfavorable response from him about your actions. He will be less likely to berate you for going above him if your memo was full of praise regarding the encouragement he gave you. Alternatively, simply make sure that you bump into your boss's boss, and casually mention your achievement to him.

SUMMARY

In this chapter we have looked at how to manage three of the worst kinds of boss—the bosses from hell. With the bully boss and sexually harassing boss, there is some protection in employment law to draw upon, but with the glory-stealing boss, you will have to rely on your own reserves to manage the situation. In the following chapter, we will look at solutions to common problems with the boss at work.

Chapter 7

Managing the Boss—Common Problems

By this time, you should be well equipped to manage your boss in most everyday situations—and a few of the rare situations too. Most of what has been discussed so far has been concerned with *proactive boss management*—making conscious efforts to improve your relationship with your boss. However, there are many common problems that most employees will encounter at some point in their working lives that require a more *reactive* approach, that is, they will need action only as and when the situation occurs. In this chapter we will discuss solutions to these common problems.

1. My boss relies on me too much.

2. I am better at the job than my boss.

3. My boss is having an affair and I have to cover for her.

4. My boss expects me to run errands for her.

5. My boss promised me a raise/promotion but it hasn't materialized.

6. My boss never tells me what's going on.

7. My boss doesn't seem to like me.

8. My boss used to be my colleague—I can't get used to her being the boss.

9. My boss is a control freak.

MY BOSS RELIES ON ME TOO MUCH

This is a common situation experienced by many administrative assistants and secretaries, but could happen to anyone. The whole point of your boss being the boss is that she gets to delegate work to you and, in extreme cases, have you do the work while she manages the process. It is only a small jump from delegation to total reliance. Your boss may rely on you too much if

◆ she is always asking your advice.

◆ she always expects you to stay late when she does, to help her out.

◆ you have to prepare all her presentations for her.

◆ she calls you at home or on your vacations.

◆ you find that you are not only doing the work, but managing too.

◆ you are doing more work than your boss.

◆ you organize her work life for her.

◆ she tries to block any ideas you have of moving on.

On the one hand, having your boss rely on you so much can be beneficial to you—making yourself indispensable is a good way to resist downsizing and to strengthen your bargaining position for a raise. However, it could soon end up that you are trapped in a gilded cage—well paid, but unable to move up. Your boss may be so unwilling for you to leave that she goes so far as to block promotion prospects. If you think you are in danger of having a boss rely on you too much, follow these guidelines.

◆ *Step 1.* Try to reduce her reliance on you. Do this by showing her how to do some of the tasks you do. Explain that she should know how to do them in case you are ill or unavailable. When projects are discussed, ensure a division of labor by stating that you will do x, y, and z if she does a, b, and c.

◆ *Step 2.* Ensure that your prospects are not blocked. If you do decide it's time to move on, reassure your boss that you will help train your successor and that you won't leave her in the lurch.

◆ *Step 3.* Be firm when you are on vacation. Make sure you take all your time off and train your boss well in terms of dealing with things in your absence. Then, *don't* give her your contact numbers. And, don't call in either!

I AM BETTER AT THE JOB THAN MY BOSS

This is a very different problem from being relied upon too much and requires rather different management. Whereas the overreliant boss recognizes and accepts your skills, the "not-as-good-as-me" boss usually does not, and if she does, she is likely (quite naturally) to feel threatened. It often takes a specific trigger for an employee to realize that she is better at the job than her boss. Such triggers commonly include

◆ covering the boss for maternity leave/sick leave, and realizing that you did a better job than she did.

◆ repeated higher achievements than your boss—more sales, awards, publications, and so on.

◆ realization that others come to you for advice/help—not to your boss

The trick to managing this boss is to subtly reassure her that her job is not at risk (even if it is) while ensuring your own deserved advancement—a difficult balance! Quite clearly, if you can do the job better than the boss, then you should be aiming for promotion—to her position or the equivalent. However, this does not mean that you should be trying to replace your boss. On the contrary, people move up much more quickly these days than in the days of a "job for life," except, perhaps, in some older, more traditional industries, so keeping good relations with your boss may ensure that she recommends you as her successor. If you do expect your boss to move up in the next couple of years, be patient, bury your frustration, and make sure she knows what an ideal successor you would be.

But what if your boss has been there for years, and is likely to stay until retirement—and she's only 40? In this case, you might be better off looking for advancement elsewhere in the company or with a different organization or company. You will need to follow the tips in the rest of this book to make sure you stay on good terms with your boss so that she gives you an excellent reference.

MY BOSS IS HAVING AN AFFAIR AND I HAVE TO COVER FOR HER

This is a very tricky situation made worse by the following circumstances:

◆ You know/are friendly with the boss's spouse.

◆ You are asked to lie to the spouse.

◆ You are expected to lie to other people at work.

How do you manage this boss? Do you lie and keep your boss happy, or refuse to cover for her and risk her wrath—and the consequences of that for your career? The answer depends, in part, on your attitude about the whole thing. Some people have the view that what their boss (or anyone else) is up to is not their concern, and refuse to moralize. If you are happy to cover for your boss when her spouse calls, then go ahead. However, many people do feel uncomfortable with lying to anyone, especially the partner of someone having an affair. Use the following guide to try to manage a cheating boss.

◆ *Step 1.* Sit down with your boss and explain to her how uncomfortable lying makes you feel without actually refusing to do it. Ask her if there is another way; perhaps she could persuade her partner not to call her at work, or maybe she would agree to lie to *you* about her whereabouts.

◆ *Step 2.* Resist the urge to moralize or lecture. You may be within your rights to not lie, but it is not your place to teach your boss right from wrong—which she is probably well aware of anyway.

◆ *Step 3.* If you cannot reach an agreement with your boss over this, you will have to decide what matters more to you—your current job or a blemish on your integrity. It might be that if you can ride it out, the affair will end soon, but if not, you may want to think about moving on. After all, you may no longer want to work for someone who not only lies and cheats on her partner, but doesn't respect your wish not to be involved.

MY BOSS EXPECTS ME TO RUN ERRANDS FOR HER

It's one thing to run out for the occasional sandwich for your boss, but it's quite another to be expected to pick up her dry cleaning, buy a birthday present for her partner, book theater tickets, and do her Christmas shopping for her. However, in managing this kind of boss, it is important to weigh a number of considerations. Ask yourself these questions.

What is my job title?

An administrative assistant could reasonably be expected to do some personal errands if it frees time for the boss to concentrate on her job. But, it is less reasonable to expect this of an assistant marketing manager, for example.

Is my boss otherwise reasonable?

If so, perhaps you could put up with the errand running as a minor irritation.

Am I gaining valuable experience/training in this job?

It is definitely worth putting up with these inconveniences if, in the grand scale of things, you are advancing your career.

Does the time involved in running errands eat into the time I have available for doing my job?

If so, this suggests that the errand running is getting out of hand.

Am I having to stay late to fit in her errands and my own work?

You definitely need to tackle your boss!

If, having asked yourself these questions, you decide that you cannot be quiet for much longer, it is time to approach your boss. The angle to take is the infringement on your work quality that running her errands is producing. Explain that, while you are happy to run the occasional errand, you are being paid to do another job and you are unable to do it justice when you are constantly interrupted to do things that are not part of your job description. Your boss may not be aware of just how much time you do spend on her errands, so it might be useful to keep a time sheet so she can see that the "occasional" errand is actually taking up more than five hours a week.

MY BOSS PROMISED ME A RAISE/PROMOTION BUT IT HASN'T MATERIALIZED

This is a surprisingly common problem. The boss implicitly or explicitly leads you to believe that a raise or promotion will be yours, only to "forget" having ever promised it—or to maintain that you misunderstood. Usually, the promise is in return for your working late or completing a job particularly well. Or it is a promise made in order to retain you through turbulent or difficult times.

If this has happened to you, there is little you can do *this time* to force your boss's hand, but you can learn from the experience. The next time you are made any kind of promise, follow this guide.

◆ *Step 1.* Make it explicit. Promises of raises or promotions are often implied suggestions, such as, "If we win this contract, I'll take care of you" or "It will be very much in your interest to complete this project." It is important to make these suggestions explicit by asking for clarification. Ask your boss exactly what she means by "in your interest" or "take care of you." If she is vague about it ask if this means a raise or promotion. Ask what kind of promotion or what sort of number the raise would be.

◆ *Step 2*. Put it in writing. Send a (dated) memo to your boss in which you express your delight at being offered the raise/promotion to be awarded at the end of the project/when the particular job is completed.

◆ *Step 3*. Follow up. Once the job is completed—or whatever you had to do before the offered raise was to be awarded—ask your boss for what was promised.

MY BOSS NEVER TELLS ME WHAT'S GOING ON

Your boss is not, of course, obligated to tell you everything that is going on, but it does make your work life more pleasant if you are kept informed of the things that affect you. Your boss may be unreasonably keeping things from you if

◆ you are suddenly moved to a different office with no prior warning.

◆ you see an ad in the paper for a new position in your company—working alongside you.

◆ there are rumors of a merger but your boss doesn't say anything.

◆ you hear important things from the grapevine before you do from your boss.

◆ people in other departments know more about company changes than you do.

The best way to manage the information-retentive boss is to join forces with your coworkers, since they are likely to be just as irritated. If you cannot get others to join you—perhaps you are in

a small company or department—then you can still go it alone. Either way, the following guide should help.

◆ *Step 1.* Gather some evidence. Complaining vaguely to your boss about not being kept informed won't carry much weight, but if you can give several examples of incidents when you were not told about something—that you feel was unreasonably withheld—you will have a stronger case.

◆ *Step 2.* Explain why you are bothered. Some withholding of information can simply be irritating but there are occasions when it can make a practical difference. You should tell your boss how you feel and the result that the lack of information has had on your morale, work output, or modus operandi; for instance, perhaps if you had known about something you could have prepared in advance and therefore wasted less work time.

◆ *Step 3.* Emphasize the positives. Try to avoid simply presenting your boss with criticism. Explain that you are very enthusiastic about the way she does something else, such as assigns work, gives feedback, etc. This should greatly increase your chances of success.

MY BOSS DOESN'T SEEM TO LIKE ME

Your boss does not have to like you. As long as she respects the job you do, she does not have to want to be your best friend. However, we all know that it can help enormously if your boss *does* like you because she will be more likely to

◆ do favors for you.

◆ grant your requests.

◆ make allowances when necessary.

◆ make your working conditions pleasant.

◆ give you desirable jobs.

How do you know if your boss does not like you? Most of us instinctively know when someone dislikes us, but here are some clues to look for.

◆ She doesn't smile at you (but she does at your colleagues).

◆ She seems irritated by you.

◆ She seems to avoid you.

◆ She gives you the least desirable jobs.

◆ She rarely grants requests or favors.

The best way to manage this boss is to try to find out what it is that she dislikes about you. But, be warned! This honesty should be sought only if you can take it.

Rather than ask your boss straight out why she dislikes you, which is certain to elicit denials from her because no one wants to be downright offensive, it is more effective to ask her if there is anything that you are doing—or not doing—that she would rather were different. The best time to ask this is at your yearly evaluation, but if yours is a long way off, you could find another opportunity to ask it. If your boss is reluctant to be drawn into a discussion of your faults, help her out by making a couple of suggestions. If you do manage to coax the reason, see if you can change whatever it is that is causing the problem. In the end, however, it could just be a personality clash between the two of you and you may have to accept this—or move on.

MY BOSS USED TO BE MY COLLEAGUE—I CAN'T GET USED TO HER BEING MY BOSS!

There are all sorts of issues tied up in this problem. It is almost invariable that at some time in your working life, a colleague will be promoted and become your superior. This can be difficult for both of you to cope with. You may feel jealous and resentful that she was promoted over you. She, on the other hand, may find it tough to be a boss while not appearing to be lording it over former friends and colleagues. This plan should guide you.

◆ *Step 1.* She is the boss now—get used to it! Any feelings of resentment you have must be swallowed or put to one side; they are destructive and your career could suffer. Maybe your colleague did not deserve the promotion; there's nothing you can do about it so you may as well keep quiet about it. Attempting to sabotage your new boss's progress is more likely to backfire on you.

◆ *Step* 2. Be honest. Tell your new boss how awkward you feel with the new balance of power. The chances are she probably feels the same. Once these feelings are out in the open, you can discuss and agree to new ground rules, such as whether you will continue to eat together in the cafeteria, drink together after work, and so on.

◆ *Step* 3. Be on her side. The best way to manage this particular boss is to help her and generally be there for her. She will probably be finding the transition difficult too and will be forever grateful to you for making life easier at this time.

◆ *Step* 4. Don't be too chummy. Be very careful not to go too far in your attempts to keep on the good side of your new boss. Being too friendly can have its downside as work and social boundaries become blurred. A pal who is your boss can easily take advantage of you by asking you to do "favors," such as continually working late or on weekends. You will find it harder to say No than you would to a boss who was never your friend socially. It is important for both of you to maintain a business separation, even if this is something that can be switched off at the end of the working day.

MY BOSS IS A CONTROL FREAK
You know your boss is a control freak when

◆ she finds it almost impossible to delegate.

◆ she is so involved with your work that she might as well be doing it herself.

◆ she wants to know *everything* that you are doing.

◆ she insists on everything being done her way.

◆ she calls in three times a day from her vacation.

◆ she rarely takes her full vacation.

◆ she wants constant reports from you.

The only way to manage the control freak boss is to build up her confidence by playing to her obsession. The controlling boss is terrified to let go, because if she does, her world might fall apart. You need to convince her that this will not be so, that not only will her world continue to function, but that it will function very well. You will be able to achieve this only through time and by using the following tips.

◆ Preempt the boss's need to check up on you by supplying regular reports and updates.

◆ Keep in regular communication with your boss so she doesn't need to contact you.

◆ Do the work exactly the way the boss tells you—resist introducing your own way of doing things (yet).

◆ Don't pester for or demand more freedom.

◆ Make sure you know the exact status of projects so that you can tell the boss when she asks.

◆ Do work in a logical fashion that will appeal to your boss's need for order.

If you follow these tips for several months (or longer), your boss may eventually learn to trust you. Control freaks often have one or two people they feel it is safe to delegate to, but once you become one of them, be sure to continue to act as before. The only difference is that you might be able to start suggesting or introducing small changes. The controlling boss is not afraid of change, only of being out of control, so make sure any change involves and includes her—even better if you can make her think it was her idea!

SUMMARY

We have concluded by looking at nine common problems with managing your boss. If these situations are dealt with in the proper way, a potential negative can be turned into a positive—with your boss being more impressed with you than ever. This, after all, is surely the art of managing your boss!

Index

◆